MILITARY MACHINES

AIRCRAFT CARRIERS

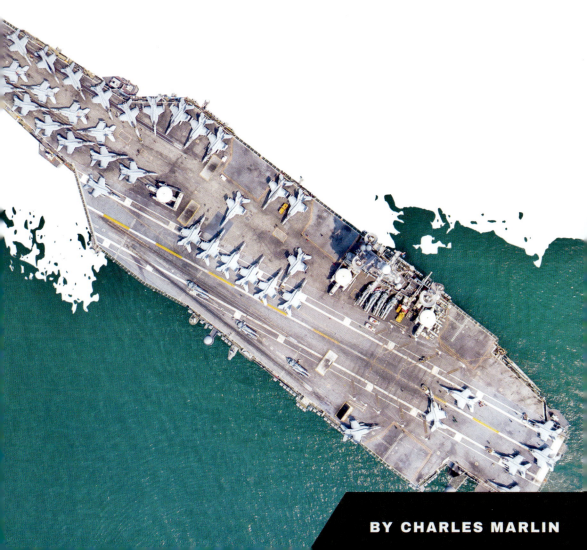

BY CHARLES MARLIN

WWW.APEXEDITIONS.COM

Copyright © 2025 by Apex Editions, Mendota Heights, MN 55120. All rights reserved. No part of this book may be reproduced or utilized in any form or by any means without written permission from the publisher.

Apex is distributed by North Star Editions:
sales@northstareditions.com | 888-417-0195

Produced for Apex by Red Line Editorial.

Photographs ©: Mass Communication Specialist 2nd Class Ruben Reed/US Navy/DVIDS, cover; iStockphoto, 1, 9; Mass Communication Specialist 3rd Class Brandon Roberson/US Navy/DVIDS, 4–5; Shutterstock Images, 6–7, 13, 14–15; Petty Officer 1st Class Ryan G. Wilber/US Navy/DVIDS, 8; PhotoQuest/Archive Photos/Getty Images, 10–11; DVIDS, 12, 22–23; Mass Communication Specialist 2nd Class Nicholas A. Russell/US Navy/DVIDS, 16–17, 29; Steve Helber/AP Images, 18; Darin Russell/US Navy/DVIDS, 19; Mass Communication Specialist 3rd Class Oswald Felix Jr./US Navy/DVIDS, 20–21; Mass Communication Specialist 3rd Class Grant G. Grady/US Navy/DVIDS, 24; Mass Communication Specialist 2nd Class Sean M. Castellano/US Navy/DVIDS, 25; Mass Communication Specialist 2nd Class Justin McTaggart/US Navy/DVIDS, 26–27

Library of Congress Control Number: 2024940123

ISBN
979-8-89250-334-1 (hardcover)
979-8-89250-372-3 (paperback)
979-8-89250-444-7 (ebook pdf)
979-8-89250-410-2 (hosted ebook)

Printed in the United States of America
Mankato, MN
012025

NOTE TO PARENTS AND EDUCATORS

Apex books are designed to build literacy skills in striving readers. Exciting, high-interest content attracts and holds readers' attention. The text is carefully leveled to allow students to achieve success quickly. Additional features, such as bolded glossary words for difficult terms, help build comprehension.

CHAPTER 1
AIR AND SEA 4

CHAPTER 2
HISTORY 10

CHAPTER 3
TRICKY TAKEOFFS 16

CHAPTER 4
OCEAN BASE 22

COMPREHENSION QUESTIONS • 28
GLOSSARY • 30
TO LEARN MORE • 31
ABOUT THE AUTHOR • 31
INDEX • 32

CHAPTER 1

AIR AND SEA

A flight crew guides a jet. The plane moves across an aircraft carrier's deck. The jet's engines rumble. It speeds down the **runway**. It flies off the ship's edge.

An aircraft carrier usually has thousands of flight crew members.

The jet soars into the air. It flies toward an enemy base. Meanwhile, the flight crew begins to send off another plane.

FAST FACT
Some carriers can **launch** an aircraft every 20 seconds.

Large aircraft carriers may hold up to 90 aircraft on board.

After a plane lands, crews chain it to the carrier's deck.

The planes attack the enemy base together. Then they return to the carrier. They take turns landing. The flight crew quickly moves each plane off the landing strip.

MULTIPLE RUNWAYS

Takeoff runways are straight. But landing strips angle across carriers. The strips point away from people and other planes. That way, planes can take off again if they have problems landing.

Landing strips are only about 500 feet (150 m) long.

CHAPTER 2

History

People began landing planes at sea in the early 1910s. Navies built **platforms** atop ships. By the early 1920s, several navies had aircraft carriers.

The US Navy made its first aircraft carrier in 1922. The ship was called the USS *Langley*

Navies first used carriers for battle during World War II (1939–1945). Carriers helped with long-range attacks. Planes could reach targets more than 200 miles (320 km) away.

Aircraft carriers used in World War II had a single runway for landing and taking off.

Japan's navy destroyed 3 US ships and 188 airplanes at Pearl Harbor. Carriers played a key part in this attack.

PEARL HARBOR

On December 7, 1941, Japan attacked Pearl Harbor in Hawai'i. The attack used six carriers. About 360 planes took off from their decks. The planes flew 275 miles (443 km).

FAST FACT

By the 1950s, some carriers had **missile** launchers. They could take down enemy planes.

14

Aircraft carriers changed after World War II. New carriers had two runways. And many began using **nuclear** power.

Nuclear power could move larger carriers. It also helped ships carry more fuel and weapons.

15

CHAPTER 3

Tricky Takeoffs

Today, aircraft carriers move jet planes. Jets take off and land at high speeds. They need space to change speed. So, many carrier decks are more than 1,000 feet (300 m) long.

When a jet begins landing, it may be going 150 miles per hour (241 km/h)

Most carriers use steam to power catapults.

To launch planes, carriers can use **catapults**. A catapult shoots a small shuttle along a track. The shuttle connects to a plane. It helps the plane quickly speed up while taking off.

FAST FACT
Some aircraft carriers use ramps instead of catapults.

Ramps cost less than catapults. But they can only launch smaller planes.

Steel cables stretch across landing runways. Each plane has a tailhook. During landings, the pilot must hook the plane to a cable. That slows the plane.

CATCHING CABLES

Most carriers have four cables for landings. To catch a cable, pilots must land at just the right angle. Mirrors and lights on the deck help pilots steer.

When landing, pilots speed up. If their tailhook misses the cables, they can take off again.

CHAPTER 4

OCEAN BASE

Aircraft carriers act like moving bases. The ships can travel around the world. Some help navies keep peace. Others help fight.

Aircraft carriers can travel about 800 miles (1,300 km) in a day.

Hangar bays below a carrier's deck store planes. Big elevators move planes down to these areas.

Some battles take place at sea. Carriers help attack enemy ships or planes. Or carriers send planes to fight targets on land.

FAST FACT
Aircraft carriers travel in a **fleet**. Other ships **protect** carriers from enemies.

Cruisers and destroyers often travel with aircraft carriers. These smaller ships guard against attacks.

People run each carrier from a tower above the deck. Workers on one level control the ship. People on another level tell planes where to go.

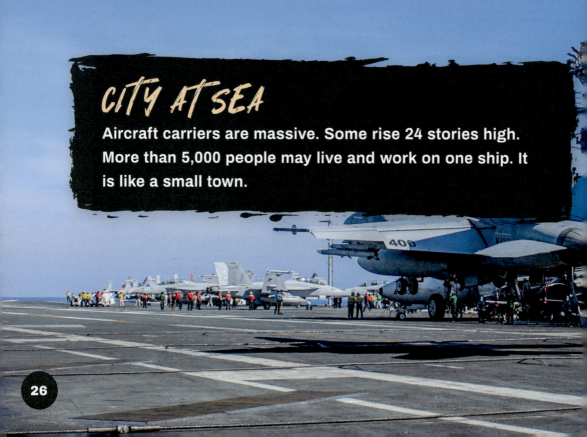

CITY AT SEA

Aircraft carriers are massive. Some rise 24 stories high. More than 5,000 people may live and work on one ship. It is like a small town.

The control tower is built near the edge of a carrier's deck. That makes room for planes to land.

COMPREHENSION QUESTIONS

Write your answers on a separate piece of paper.

1. Write a few sentences describing the main ideas of Chapter 2.

2. Would you like to work on an aircraft carrier? Why or why not?

3. In what year did the attack on Pearl Harbor happen?
    - **A.** 1939
    - **B.** 1941
    - **C.** 1945

4. Why might aircraft carriers have four cables for landing planes?
    - **A.** so pilots can catch all four wires each time
    - **B.** so pilots do not have to aim when landing
    - **C.** so pilots can catch a different wire if they miss one

5. What does **targets** mean in this book?

*Carriers helped with long-range attacks. Planes could reach **targets** more than 200 miles (320 km) away.*

    A. places with no enemies
    B. things people plan to attack
    C. times when fighting stops

6. What does **massive** mean in this book?

*Aircraft carriers are **massive**. Some rise 24 stories high. More than 5,000 people may live and work on one ship.*

    A. large
    B. hidden
    C. small

Answer key on page 32.

GLOSSARY

catapults
Devices that help planes speed up quickly and take off from runways.

fleet
A group of warships under one command.

launch
To send something up into the air.

missile
An object that is shot or launched as a weapon.

nuclear
Having to do with parts of the tiny bits of matter called atoms.

platforms
Raised, flat surfaces.

protect
To keep something or someone safe.

runway
A flat strip where aircraft can take off and land.

BOOKS

Bassier, Emma. *Military Aircraft*. Minneapolis: Abdo Publishing, 2020.

Bolte, Mari. *Aircraft Carriers in Action.* Minneapolis: Lerner Publications, 2024.

Storm, Ashley. *US Navy*. Mendota Heights, MN: Apex Editions, 2023.

ONLINE RESOURCES

Visit **www.apexeditions.com** to find links and resources related to this title.

ABOUT THE AUTHOR

Charles Marlin is an author, editor, and avid cyclist. He lives in rural Iowa.

C
crew, 4, 6, 8

F
fleet, 25

J
Japan, 13

L
landings, 8–9, 10, 16, 20–21

N
navies, 10, 12, 22
nuclear, 15

P
Pearl Harbor, 13
planes, 4, 6, 8–9, 10, 12–14, 16, 18, 20, 24, 26

R
runways, 4, 9, 15, 20

S
ships, 4, 10, 15, 22, 24–26

T
tailhook, 20
tower, 26

W
World War II, 12, 15

ANSWER KEY:
1. Answers will vary; 2. Answers will vary; 3. B; 4. C; 5. B; 6. A